Alligators

Ashley Lee

Explore other books at:
WWW.ENGAGEBOOKS.COM

VANCOUVER, B.C.

WWW.ENGAGEBOOKS.COM

Alligators: Pre-1
Animals That Make a Difference!
Lee, Ashley, 1995
Text © 2025 Engage Books
Design © 2025 Engage Books

Edited by: A.R. Roumanis, and Ashley Lee
Design by: Mandy Christiansen

Text set in Arial Regular.

FIRST EDITION / FIRST PRINTING

library and archives canada cataloguing in publication

Title: Alligators / Ashley Lee.
Names: Lee, Ashley, author.
Description: Series statement: Animals that make a difference

Identifiers: Canadiana (print) 20230448542 | Canadiana (ebook) 20230448569
ISBN 978-1-77878-686-0 (hardcover)
ISBN 978-1-77878-695-2 (softcover)

Subjects:
LCSH: Alligators—Juvenile literature.
LCSH: Human-animal relationships—Juvenile literature.

Classification: LCC QL737.P94 C38 2025 | DDC J599.885—DC23

This project has been made possible in part
by the Government of Canada.

Canada

Don't get too close!

Alligators have short legs.

Their tails are very strong.

Alligators are covered in hard scales.

Scales

Scales keep alligators
safe from other alligators.

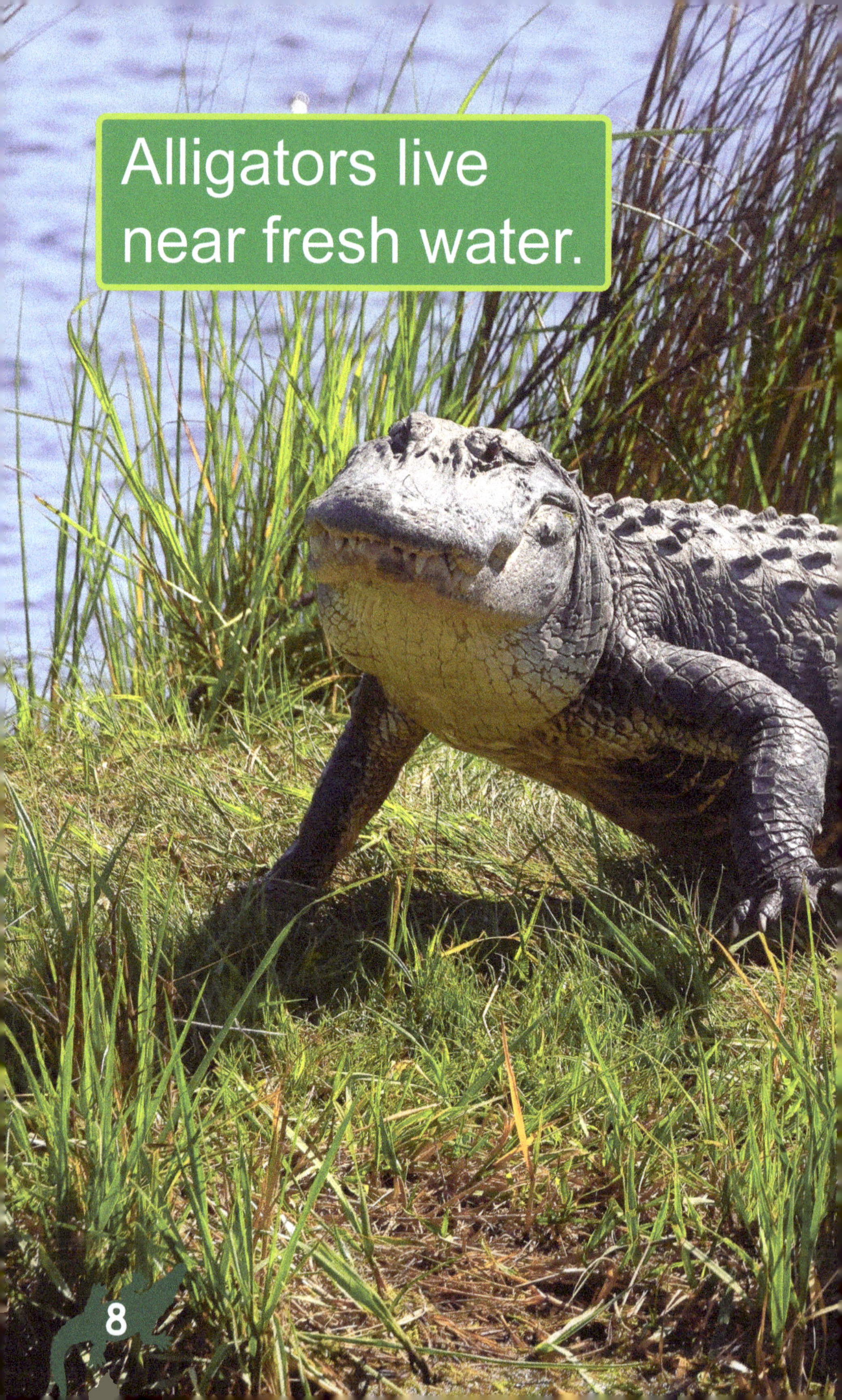

Alligators live near fresh water.

Fresh water is not salty.

Most alligators live in America.

A few live in China.

Some alligators can stay underwater for more than an hour.

Alligators eat other animals.

They like fish,
frogs, and birds.

Eating other animals helps alligators keep Earth healthy.

Too many animals in one place can hurt the Earth.

Alligators make sure
this does not happen.

Baby alligators are food for some animals.

Other animals would go hungry without them.

Alligators dig holes in the ground.

These holes keep them safe from bad weather.

Alligator holes often have water in them.

They can be homes for other animals.

Alligators lay eggs in nests.

There can be 30 to
70 eggs in one nest.

Baby alligators leave home after two or three years.

They live for about
50 years.

Quiz

Test your knowledge of alligators by answering the following questions. The questions are based on what you have read in this book. The answers are listed on the bottom of the next page.

1 Do alligators have short legs?

2 Do alligators live near fresh water?

3 Do alligators eat other animals?

4 Are baby alligators food for some animals?

5 Do alligators dig holes in the ground?

6 Do alligators lay eggs in nests?

Explore other books in the
Animals That Make a Difference series

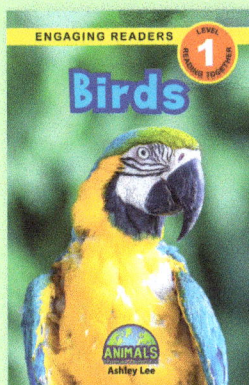

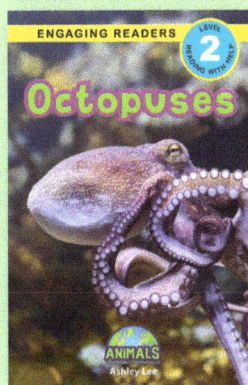

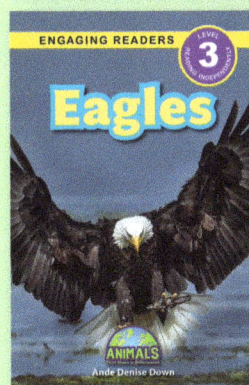
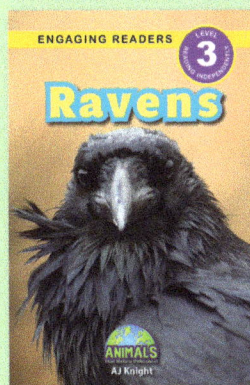
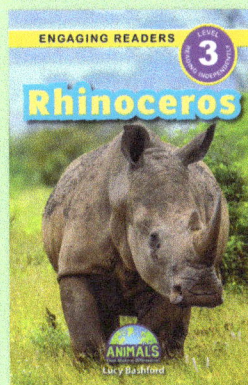

Visit www.engagebooks.com to explore more Engaging Readers.

www.ingramcontent.com/pod-product-compliance
Lightning Source LLC
Chambersburg PA
CBHW052035030426
42337CB00027B/5010